Advan
A Professional Guide

MW01601114

"Finally, here's a battle-tested guide for all professionals that will enable them to win against today's tough competition. It's a 'must read' before you go to your next beauty contest."

THOMAS E. WAGNER, VICE CHAIRMAN
CALFEE, HALTER & GRISWOLD LLP

"George Havens helped us tremendously. I first called him after hearing one of his award-winning presentations. I was so impressed I asked him to teach us how to adapt his principles. He's the ultimate professional."

MARIA KECKAN, PRESIDENT, CINECRAFT PRODUCTIONS, INC.

"There's nothing academic or ivory tower about this guide. It's based on the street smarts that George Havens acquired as he became an expert in winning presentations."

SCOTT S. COWEN, PRESIDENT, TULANE UNIVERSITY,
FORMER DEAN, WEATHERHEAD SCHOOL OF MANAGEMENT

"George Havens reveals all the secrets he utilized in creating one of Cleveland's fastest-growing ad agencies. Every marketing professional should devour this guide... your competitors surely will."

CHARLES R. EMRICK JR., VICE PRESIDENT/ PRINICIPAL
THE TRANSACTION GROUP

"Winning a competitive presentation is getting tougher every day... but it will be easier with the best practices that George Havens presents so clearly and precisely in his new book. If you're serious about success, you need this book."

RICHARD J. SEMENIK, PH.D., DEAN, COLLEGE OF BUSINESS,
MONTANA STATE UNIVERSITY, AUTHOR OF *Advertising &
Integrated Brand Promotion* AND *Promotion & Integrated
Marketing Communications*

"Professionals who want to lead with their best foot forward will find this down-to-earth guide invaluable. George Havens really knows his stuff!"

JAMIE WILLIAMS, STATE DIRECTOR
THE NATURE CONSERVATORY OF MONTANA

A Professional Guide to

WINNING
PRESENTATIONS

SURE-FIRE STRATEGIES AND TACTICS
FOR A SUCCESSFUL PITCH

George N. Havens

©2003 George Havens

ISBN: 1-929774-24-9

Cover and Layout by Francine Smith

Submit all requests for reprinting to:
Greenleaf Book Group LLC
8227 Washington Street, Suite #2, Chagrin Falls, OH 44023

Published in the United States by
Greenleaf Book Group LLC, Cleveland, Ohio.

www.greenleafbookgroup.com

Preface

This Guide is designed for the *hunters* in an organization.

Since nothing really happens until a sale is made, hunters play an indispensable role in the survival and success of the firm. Hunters thrill to the chase, are highly competitive, and derive their rewards from winning. They are fundamentally different from *harvesters* who with complementary skills know how to service and satisfy clients on an ongoing basis.

Every organization needs both hunters and harvesters, but without victorious hunters there will be nothing to harvest. Thus, the Guide focuses on how to help hunters win their competitive pitches.

I need to express my appreciation to those who have contributed to the development of this Guide. A number of people reviewed and critiqued the manuscript: Stanley F. Meyer, former CEO of Wendt Advertising; Dr. Richard Semenik, dean, College of Business, Montana State University; Peter Havens, group executive with BNP Publishing; and Jack Warner, former CEO of Warner, Bicking & Fenwick Advertising. My former colleagues in The Jayme Organization and in the Transworld Advertising Agency Network will recognize some of their ideas and inspiration in the Guide.

Clinton Greenleaf in his role as publisher was a partner in originating the concept of the Guide and directing its realization. Virginia Havens, my wife and an English teacher, afforded me invaluable support, encouragement and on-target critiques. All enhanced this Guide but any mistakes or inaccuracies are totally my responsibility.

My sincere wish is that you will find this Guide valuable, use it in good health, win an increasing percentage of your presentations, and have some fun along the way.

George N. Havens
Bozeman, Montana

Dedicated to all my clients
who said "Yes"
and to my colleagues
who shared the victory celebrations.

Contents

How to get ready

Before you dig into the strategies and tactics of winning presentations, consider these basic realities:

- *A competitive presentation is not simply an exercise in public speaking. It requires a specialized skill with one objective: to win.*

- *Strong presentation skills are always an essential requisite for the top-drawer professional or executive.*

- *Mental and psychological preparation is just as important as the actual presentation content.*

- *Typical of most business endeavors, a set of best practices for presentations have evolved and they provide the competitive edge.*

  As in any competitive contest, the command is "Get Ready!"

Introduction

Public speaking and *competitive presentations* — they're different.

Public speaking takes many forms. Teaching in a classroom, seminar or workshop. Campaign oratory. Motivational speaking. Coaching. Presenting a point of view. Lecturing. Political debating. Giving a report. Even stand-up comedy. Note the differing objectives: to educate, persuade, motivate, coach, inform, update, amuse.

Competitive presentations usually are stand-up pitches. They have a singular objective: to win.

Public speaking is usually a solo event. *Competitive presentations* may involve an individual or a team.

Public speaking audiences may vary widely in intelligence, background, prejudices, knowledge of the subject, demographics, and level of interest. *Competitive presentations* are typically made to an audience that's serious, savvy, sophisticated, skeptical, and seeking to make a Yes or No decision.

Public speaking is normally a monologue with limited opportunity for questions and discussion. *Competitive presentations* encourage questions and seek to surface doubts, negatives and buyer resistances.

Public speakers often receive a flowery introduction which establishes their expertise. *Competitive presenters* have to introduce themselves and create their own credibility.

Public speakers frequently use a canned presentation or do their "schtick." *Competitive presenters* must customize their pitch to the needs, wants and expectations of each audience.

Not all public speakers know how to give a winning presentation. All *competitive presenters* must be competent public speakers.

Yes, they're different. That's why this guide exists.

Advance warning

Bet on it. It's going to happen to you.

Sooner or later if you're on an upward track in a vital organization, you'll be asked to give a competitive presentation. Likely, it will be sooner and you'll need to be *ready*.

You may be doing a new business pitch, leading a professional service firm "beauty contest," proposing a new initiative to your own top management, or securing a critical contract or commitment.

The outcome of *your* presentation will affect your self-esteem and the opinion of your peers, your next raise or the trajectory of your career, perhaps the success of your team or the survival of your organization, and most certainly whether your point of view prevails. So it is imperative, for all these reasons, that you give an effective presentation.

This guide will show you how to give a winning presentation. Like the innovative play book that Coach Paul Brown introduced to professional football, these rules will give you a competitive edge over your rivals. The guide won't guarantee success, but it will leverage your natural abilities and improve your odds immensely.

This is not a general book on public speaking. There are dozens of those. This is a book on how to win when the chips are down and the stakes are high, when the competition is tough and you need to be at the top of your game. The practices presented here have been proved in the trenches over many years. Learn them. Use them. Then get ready to celebrate your victory.

Upfront preparation

Before you show up for your presentation, here's how to prepare yourself.

1. Bring your competitive spirit with you. If you don't want to win so badly that you can taste it, you probably won't.

2. Get psyched up. A Hall of Fame pro quarterback* used to throw up before each game. You don't have to go that far and you don't have to be an adrenaline junkie, but get ready to play at the top of your game.

3. Flush other concerns, problems and worries out of your mind. Focus laser-like on the opportunity in front of you.

4. Have a hungry attitude and a hungry body. Skip any heavy food beforehand, it'll only slow down your brain cells.

5. Adopt the winning "inner game" techique of top athletes who visualize hitting a home run or a service ace. Create a mental image of how successfully you will deliver your presentation and let your subconscious help you win.

6. Check, double check, then check again that you have all of your notes, materials, props, equipment and other essentials. Start early to get ready — have everything in place 48 hours in advance.

7. Verify the equipment you need and make sure it is available. Bring a back-up set of materials not dependent on technology.

8. If the presentation is at the prospect's place of business, plan to arrive early. Tardiness due to traffic jams and parking problems will make you a loser.

9. Infect your team members with confidence through your positive, upbeat attitude.

10. Turn off your cell phone and/or pager. Your audience expects 100% concentration on them.

11. Relax. You can't think straight, talk convincingly or project a professional image if you're uptight.

12. Expect the best of yourself. Visualize how great it will be to win. Turn on your "internal teleprompter." Then do your stuff.

* *Otto Graham of the Cleveland Browns*

Best practices

The best practices in this guide have been battle-tested.

I spent my professional career in the advertising agency business, the last 15 as president and then CEO of the fastest-growing agency in Cleveland. During that period our firm's income became ten times larger despite intense competition from larger agencies in our marketplace and national agencies from New York, Detroit and Chicago. We beat some of the best.

New business is the lifeblood of an ad agency, so you learn fast how to win or the firm goes down the tube. We learned by losing new business pitches, then finding out why we lost. By experimenting with novel approaches. By finding ways to make our *intangible* services *tangible.* By racheting up sensitivity to our audiences. By adapting successful techniques used by affiliate agencies in our international network. By truly adopting the prospect's point of view. By spending long days and evenings in preparation for the showdown event.

What evolved out of this process were the winning presentation practices prescribed in this guide. Utilizing these techniques our agency won close to 50% of the new business clients that we really lusted after — as good as it gets in the ad game. And the CEO of a major Cleveland corporation rated us as "one of the two most innovative agencies" he knew.

This means that you can rely on these presentation rules to work for you. They are applicable to one-on-one or one-on-many presentations. They can be effective for all types of professional service firms and many other organizations — wherever a competitive pitch must be made.

So read on.

How to deliver a winning pitch

Here in 20 brief statements are the practical principles and game plan strategies for giving a successful pitch.

Read them. Reflect on them. Absorb them. Adopt those that will enhance your natural presentation abilities. But always integrate them with your own inimitable and personal style.

These Rules can make you a winner. But only if you perform at the top of your game and execute them flawlessly.

Rule No. 1

Analyze your audience

Each individual in your audience will arrive with different motivations. The more you understand these motivations, the greater your chances for success.

Your preparation should include digging into the background, responsibilities, position and perspectives of each individual as well as their non-business interests and activities. Try to meet with them beforehand. Then you can gear your presentation to these factors. Speaking to "strangers" sharply reduces your odds for success.

Go to school on their organization so that you can:

- Allude to their customers
- Recognize their competitiors
- Know the environment they compete in.

It helps if you scope out "who wants what." A financial officer may be concerned about bottom-line impact. A president may focus on overall company image. A marketing manager on competitive reactions. A human resources person on staffing issues. To win their votes you must clarify and reassure how your proposition will meet these disparate concerns.

Build in material that connects with the personal interests of the decision-makers. If you know that a key person is an avid golfer or tennis player, or interested in opera or charitable work, include an allusion to that interest. This creates a feeling of mutuality, touches a shared interest and provides a subtle compliment.

Employ the language of your audience. Avoid the mystifying jargon of *your* field. If you're presenting to engineers or a technical group, use graphs, diagrams, even formulas — that's their language. If you're pitching to a top-executive team, use management concepts and business vernacular.

Boil down your remarks to the information your audience *needs to know* to make a positive decision in your favor. This is not an ego exercise — quash the temptation to show them how much *you know*. That's a loser's tactic. The rule is: Think straight. Talk to the point. Shut up.

In his Second Treatise On Rhetoric, Aristotle stressed the need to "understand your audience." After several millennia, it's still sound advice.

RULE NO. 2

Plan your presentation

When you finally get the opportunity to make a presentation, go all out.

It may have taken months or years of "subtle seduction" to reach this critical juncture, so anything less than a full-bore attack is foolish. But your attack needs a written plan based on your analysis of what it will take to win.

Start with objectives. Be specific on what you want to achieve, such as:

- Secure the business on your terms (whatever they may be).
- Structure the engagement for maximum profits.
- Create the basis for a long-term working relationship.
- Secure only selected parts of the business.
- Nullify the advantages of your strongest rivals.
- Establish the basis for getting additional business downstream.

Strategies answer the question of "how" you will attain your objectives. Here you need to deal with presentation content, use of supporting graphics, timing, major appeals, focus on prospect's "hot button," handouts, added values that you will offer, and special effects. An important decision is who to include on your presentation team and who speaks (normally the fewer the better).

Then think about these implementation steps:

- Arrive early and have the room "dressed" when your audience appears.

- Create an agenda that lists the players and their positions (prospects and your presentation team) and the program — who will present what and the timing. Distribute this "program" at the start of the pitch.

- Arrange seating so people are inter-mixed. Avoid "us" vs "them" arrangements.

- Employ a brisk pace — keep the show moving.

A final caveat. Always inspect the room where you will present to get familiar with its size, shape, layout, lighting, seating, facilities, and distractions. When we omitted this vital step, our team showed up with display boards, slide and overhead projectors, screen, handouts, et al only to discover that the large conference room we planned to use was under repair. We gave an awkward, unprofessional presentation in a small crowded office.

RULE NO. 3

Put the focus on the prospect

Losers focus on themselves with lots of brag-and-boast, chest beating and puffery.

Winners concentrate on the prospects and the benefits to be gained from innovative strategies, solutions and services. In short, what's in it for them?

A top-notch presenter I know starts his pitch by paraphrasing Microsoft's slogan: Where do you want to go today? Then answers this rhetorical question as he demonstrates how his firm can aid regardless of the vector of the quest.

In structuring a typical one-hour presentation, allocate time shrewdly:

- 10 minutes to an introductory overview of your organization — capabilities, distinctive competencies, expertise, and experience. Refer them to the handout or your capabilities brochure for more comprehensive information on your firm.

- 30 minutes to your proposal
- 20 minutes to a question-and-answer segment

Devote the bulk of your time to your Point of View of the prospect:

- An analysis of its situation, problems, opportunities, threats, realities
- Research you have done on the prospect — the Internet can be a great resource here
- How you propose to enhance the success of the prospect
- How you will work together — relationship, staffing, financial
- Added values that you will uniquely provide
- Benefits to be expected from selecting your firm

A special tip: check the *Wall Street Journal* and the Internet the day of the presentation for any late-breaking news that could either enhance or invalidate your approach.

This approach has key advantages:

- No unnecessary overkill on your qualifications
- Responds to the audience's primary interest — *their* organization and *their* problems
- Showcases how you think about the prospect's situation and the excellence of your recommendations
- Helps make your *intangible* services more *tangible*

So leave your ego at home. Win by showing that you're already up-to-speed on their business, have some great ideas, and can accelerate their progress and success.

RULE NO. 4

Match your strengths to their needs

Sure, you'll construct your presentation to highlight your strengths, your core competencies, your advantages. But **how** you do it is crucial:

- Emphasize your salient capabilities that match the needs of your audience. Never offer a "laundry list" of strengths. Select them based on your prospect's "hot buttons."

- Express your strengths as customer benefits. Do not say "we have great experience in your industry." Say "you will get better results from our team because we have in-depth experience in your distribution channels."

- Position your strengths so they differentiate you from your competition. Be specific on your distinctive competencies and the unique values you can provide.

- Never claim to be everything to everybody. It's not credible and it will tarnish the rest of your presentation.

- Define the specific "fit" between you and your prospect. Why will the relationship be highly productive?

As a friend once observed: Everyone has some brooms missing from the closet. So how do you handle your weaknesses? Start by deciding whether it is a perceived weakness or a real deficiency, then handle them differently.

A perceived weakness may result from street scuttlebutt, out-of-date information or subversive comments from people who want someone else to win. Attack this situation directly with "you may have heard that we lack..." or "sometimes folks are concerned about our..." Then correct the mistaken perception with facts. Cite hard evidence that proves your case. Or refer them to your clients or users for an objective opinion.

Do not deny a real weakness, but be prepared to answer in a way that makes "lemonade out of a lemon." Some suggestions:

- "We recognize this deficiency and have launched a vigorous program to correct the problem. You'll get the benefit of that."

- "Others may have more experience in your industry. But in a fast-changing world past experience can often be a liability. What we bring is our quick-study ability so we can learn rapidly and get up-to-speed on current realities almost overnight."

- "That's not our foremost capability, but that does not appear to compromise our ability to do first-rate work for you."

- "We can't serve you in that area, but we'll help you find the best solution to that need and work with them to get you superior results."

What you need to convey is: There are good alternatives, but you offer the best "fit" between their needs and your capabilities for the optimum solution.

RULE NO. 5

Establish a common bond with your audience

You need to break the invisible barrier that exists between presenter and audience.

You can't see it, but you can feel it. And so can your audience. It will diminish your best efforts unless you break through it.

Here are some techniques that work:

- Do not use a podium. Too formal, too confining, and it's a physical barrier.
- Move up close to your audience.
- Never read your presentation. It kills spontaneity and reveals that you don't know *your* material or that it's not your material.
- Make eye contact.

- Focus on one individual at a time, then periodically shift to others around the room.

- Move around the room — a dynamic technique.

- Walk to the rear of the room as you say: "From your perspective, here is what I'd want to know about…"

Don't just talk *at* your audience. Connect with them. Get them involved. Get them excited. You're not giving a lecture, you're painting a picture of how great the future can be with the help of your organization or your proposition.

Develop your intuition and your sensitivity so that you understand what is going on in the minds of your listeners. Sense when you are talking with the grain or against it, then react accordingly.

If you can do it sincerely, compliment them on their company and its reputation. Slip in a personal reference that shows you are aware of an individual's achievements. Share a positive experience you've had with their product/service. Use a light approach that disarms and engages them.

Rule No. 6

Get off to a strong start

The old, familiar adage is that you never get a second chance to make a good first impression.

So get your presentation off to a strong start. Have the first part of your pitch down cold so it comes off like the start of a Formula One race. With a weak, sputtering opening, your presentation may die right there and never recover.

Here's a dynamic way to start that avoids some common mistakes:

- Introduce yourself — identifying your organization and your position. (I am astounded at how many presenters omit this basic requisite.)
- Introduce your team members and their positions. Add a brief word of praise for each to establish their bona fides.
- Invite your audience to introduce themselves and define

what help they are looking for. This helps break the ice
and sets the stage for a dialogue.

- Thank the audience for the opportunity to compete for
  their business and obtain their positive decision. Exude
  excitement and enthusiasm.

Next, keep your audience involved:

- State your objective for your presentation — what are
  you trying to accomplish? Sharing this with your audience adds clarity and transparency. Paraphrase it
  something like this: "Our (my) objective for this presentation is to give you all of the facts and all of the information you need to make a positive decision to select
  our firm as your new _____."

- Proclaim your value proposition: "No other firm can
  bring you the capabilities we offer you and we provide
  the best 'fit' with your needs."

- Provide a blueprint or roadmap of your presentation.
  Identify the major subject areas you will cover. Refer to
  the agenda you have provided.

- Ask the participants if there is any other information
  they would like to have. Then revise your agenda on the
  spot to dramatize your responsiveness.

- Insert "signposts" along the way. Example: "That sum-
  marizes the research we did on your markets. Next we'll
  show you how we used those findings to create a break-
  through strategy for you."

RULE NO. 7

Recognize that you always send two messages

Your audience will get two messages from you: verbal and non-verbal.

The verbal message is the obvious one, the one that you plan, prepare for and give priority to. But in many cases, your non-verbal communication is more critical to your success.

Non-verbal communication involves your conscious and unconscious body language, your dress, your overall appearance and your unintended actions and reactions. You need to recognize how crucial these factors are.

Watch a good presenter. His/her body language conveys confidence, interest, enthusiasm, energy, competence. Facial expressions are alert, open, friendly, trusting, smiling, vital.

He/she is dressed for success — stylish but conservative,

immaculate, pressed and polished (See *A Gentlemen's Guide to Appearance* by Clinton Greenleaf).

Good presenters communicate with their entire bodies. Their movements drive home key points, add emphasis, command attention, clarify meaning, provide a change of pace, or create a surprise. It all seems natural, appropriate and spontaneous. And it's essential to a winning presentation.

Work on your body movements so that they add, not distract, from your pitch. Get feedback from your colleagues. Videotape yourself. Watch professional presenters. But don't adopt rigid or planned movements, stay relaxed, natural, spontaneous.

Many presenters have trouble with their hands. Don't stand there with them in your pockets — it telegraphs lack of respect for your audience. Don't clasp them behind your back — too rigid. Just do what comes naturally to express yourself.

RULE NO. 8

Face it, you're in show biz

A dull presentation is deadly. A winning presentation will be lively, spontaneous, dramatic, full of energy and enjoyable to observe.

Employ a light touch and have some fun. It's your chance to show the audience that you are going to be great to work with.

After you have created your basic presentation, add elements from show business that are both entertaining and educational. Add some sparkle, wit and sophistication with:

- Anecdotes that drive home your point
- Quotations that make your case more memorable
- Stories that display your integrity or creativity
- Analogies that relate to the audience's experience
- A quick change of pace that perks up the group

- Even cartoons or humorous drawings to drive home a point

You can be witty or humorous, but don't tell jokes unless you are a seasoned raconteur.

Even then, the joke should be brief and support a point you wish to make. Remember what a famous playwright* said on his death bed: "Dying is easy. *Comedy* is hard."

So go "on stage." Be alive. Be animated. Be emotional. Be entertaining. Be a winner.

* *Oscar Wilde*

RULE NO. 9

Be responsive to your audience

The best presenters are always aware of what's going on with their audience.

Cultivate that sensitivity. Train yourself to watch for body language and facial expressions that tell you how you're doing. Learn the telltale signs.

When you see the following, you've got trouble:

- Whispered conversations among participants
- Restless stirring, shifting about
- Frowns, shaking of heads, skeptical expressions
- The deadly EGO — eyes glazed over
- People looking around the room, not at you

They may be tuning you out, getting bored, doubting your claims, or thinking about the next meeting. When you observe these danger signs, don't just press on. Be ready to change your pitch:

- Stop. Ask if you can clarify, substantiate or expand on any issues.
- Shorten your presentation, move quickly to the summary.
- Improvise. Do something dramatic.
- Ask a provocative question that recaptures their interest.
- Never complain or admonish — it's your problem, not theirs.

On the other hand you may receive positive feedback:

- Smiles, shared looks, nods
- Murmurs of agreement
- Close attention to your remarks
- Alert posture, receptive expressions
- Frequent taking of notes.

This is good news. Build on this dynamic. Play your strongest cards and win.

The bottom-line: Be responsive. Or get ready for the bad news.

RULE NO. 10

Provide helpful, personalized handouts

Create a high-impact written presentation that is professionally prepared and sells just as hard as your verbal pitch.

Organize it this way:

- Executive summary
- Benefits to be expected from your proposition
- Recap of your presentation (perhaps Power Point format)
- Facts about your organization
- Summary and strong "ask for the order" close
- Appendix: exhibits, reports, supporting documentation

Handouts should be *personalized* with the individual names of people invited to the presentation. Note: it is *absolutely* essential to be totally accurate on spelling of names and titles.

Create an impressive, top-quality handout through use of color, computerized graphics, charts, diagrams, eye-catching cover design, section dividers, and lay-flat binding. Check, then check again to ensure 100% correct spelling and grammar in the presentation content. Don't just rely on Spell Check — it won't catch everything.

Distribute your handouts *after* the verbal presentation. To relieve participants of the need to take detailed notes, tell them upfront that they will receive a handout at the end covering everything you will present. If a key player is absent, make sure that he/she gets a personalized copy.

All this effort is vital. Decision-makers who are absent or who are unknown to you will not witness your stand-up presentation and may make their decision based in great part on your handout.

RULE NO. 11

Prepare. Prepare. Prepare.

The key to victory is the will to prepare.

That's true in competitive sports and a presentation is fundamentally a competitive sport.

Do your homework. Dig deep for information and ideas. Be thorough. Be meticulous. There is no substitute for total preparation — and it will pay off.

A hallmark of Winston S. Churchill's great presentations in the House of Commons was the meticulous preparation that persisted throughout the whole of his career. In one instance it is recorded that he spent six weeks in preparation.

Find the "hot button" that will win the day. Learn why your predecessor is on the way out. Check your hunches with a "friend within the walls" of your target. Gain insights from other firms that serve the prospect. Do research. Analyze the prospect's previous work in your field.

Then build your presentation carefully. Run it past your colleagues who are not involved in the pitch. Record it and listen for "incredible" statements or propositions. Change it. Improve it. Polish it.

RULE NO. 12

Rehearse. Rehearse. Rehearse.

You remember the old gag which asked "How do you get to Carnegie Hall?" And the pragmatic response was "Practice. Practice. Practice."

Even the 20th century's greatest orator rehearsed religiously. Winston S. Churchill absorbed his presentations so well that as he spoke he seemed to be using an internal teleprompter. In one humorous case as he was bathing in his tub, his mutterings were so thunderous they brought his alarmed valet to his side. Churchill advised: "I wasn't talking to you, Norman. I was addressing the House of Commons."

As you rehearse your presentation (not in the tub), use your colleagues as a sounding board. Candid feedback and their reactions will help you discover the weak areas, the places where it drags, the need for better documentation, the sections that can be tightened up or deleted.

Stay flexible and be willing to revamp or rearrange your presentation until it is strong, solid, totally convincing.

As we rehearsed and re-rehearsed one crucial presentation well after midnight, we cut out one person's section which came off as marginal and uninspired. The next day we won the agency's largest account.

RULE NO. 13

Be yourself

It is useful to learn from first-rate presenters. It is appropriate to absorb the ideas in this Guide. It is productive to adopt some show business techniques.

But always be yourself. Add to your natural skills and enhance your performance, but don't try to imitate or emulate others. Trying to be someone else is uncomfortable and ineffective, even dishonest.

Perhaps the characteristic most highly desired in another individual — a superior, a colleague, a partner or an advisor — is honesty and integrity. Find a way in your own style to project those traits.

My approach was to say early in the presentation: "We want to be totally transparent to you. We want you to know how we think, how we work, how we charge, how we define success. Any question you may ask is legitimate and will get a straight answer."

The most talented competitor doesn't always win. More often it's the one who comes across as being the easiest and most rewarding to work with. Life is too short to work with someone who has poor interpersonal skills. Make it obvious that you know how to build and sustain a mutually beneficial relationship.

Critical thought: even though the prospect may "buy" you as an individual, they never want to put all of their eggs in a one-person basket. Thus, it is vital for you to reflect the personality of your organization and to stress strongly the capabilities of your organization.

RULE NO. 14

Get the most from visual aids

Visual aids can give your presentation a powerful boost in impact and memorability.

Your first decision is to decide what level of technology makes sense in the particular situation — High Tech? Low Tech? No Tech?

Here are some tips on your technology and visual format choice:

High Tech:

- Power Point is now the standard — dramatic, sophisticated, easy sequencing of content, effective use of color, ease of incorporating graphics.

- Videos (tape, CD-ROM, DVD) are excellent to show motion, commercials, history, project development, complex concepts.

Low Tech:

- Overhead transparencies have been the standard — easy to make, use and file, economical, versatile

- 35mm slides can be powerful for presenting multiple images — advertisements, site locations, past projects, designs, cityscapes, product displays, etc.

- Display boards and flip charts — limited to special uses and small groups.

No Tech:

- An intimate *personal* conversation — with or without a desktop presentation — may be just right in some circumstances.

 Here are some suggestions on use of visuals:*

- Visuals should be simple, clear, and easy to read — one idea per visual, large type, bullet-point format, use of color to accent (not camouflage), easy-to-follow design.

- Visuals should present only key points. *Never* put your full presentation on visuals and then attempt to read it.

- *Always* face the audience — talk to *them*, not to the visuals.

- If necessary, dim the room but *never* darken it — you must maintain eye contact.

- Get totally comfortable with the mechanics and operation of the equipment — not knowing how to turn on a projector or having slides backward will doom your efforts.

- Practice and rehearse with your visuals.

- Be prepared for an emergency — blown projector bulb,

missing connector cable, visuals out of order, electrical failure, equipment malfunction. Stuff happens, so be ready to save your presentation.

Remember, visuals are only an *aid* — you still need to be the star of the show.

* Manuals like *Power Point for Dummies* by Doug Lowe offer practical help in creating visual aids for various formats: Power Point, overhead, slides, Internet, handouts, etc.

RULE NO. 15

Differentiate yourself with an added value

You can make a strong presentation even stronger by emphasizing the **added value** that you will bring to the party.

The strategy here is to give them an extra reason to buy. Thus it should be something that will benefit the prospect, that you can uniquely offer, and that will differentiate your proposition. You should develop your own concept, but some practical examples are:

- Free seminar for prospect personnel on the latest trends (in the presenter's field).

- Promotional tie-ins with your other clients.

- Pro bono work for a favorite charity of the prospect.

- Software to facilitate inter-connectivity between the two parties.

- Assignment of your top client manager to the account.
- Helpful business introductions sought by prospect managers

Save this for your close. Then dramatize it by proclaiming that in addition to all the other benefits and advantages you will bring them, you have an exciting, extra, added value — which should make your firm the preferred choice.

RULE NO. 16

Conclude with a strong finish

Great symphonies end with a dramatic flourish. Sports events often end with a fireworks display. Ceremonies with a fervent benediction.

In analogous fashion you need to end your presentation with a strong, dramatic, upbeat finale:

- Summarize what you've told them
- Reinforce the benefits you can provide
- Remind that you're up-to-speed and ready to start
- Highlight the added values that you offer
- Make clear your interest and enthusiasm
- Thank your audience for the opportunity and for their attention

Then — **ask for the order!**

Finally, specify the next steps:

- Distribute the handouts
- Answer questions
- Indicate your availability to provide further information
- Volunteer to repeat the presentation for absent decision-makers
- Inquire when the decision will be made

That's it. The show is over.

RULE NO. 17

Don't overlook two decisive factors

In most of your presentations there will be intense competition. With a number of first-rate rivals there may be little to differentiate them. They will all tend to look and sound the same.

In this scenario, prospects invariably do a sensible thing: they pick the safest choice.

But there is a secret maneuver to help you win...even if you're not the safest choice.

When we asked for feedback on why we'd won many tightly-contested presentations, the typical response was — "All the firms gave excellent presentations. It was tough to choose among them. But you guys displayed more *interest in our business* and *showed more enthusiasm for working with us* than the others. Those were the deciding factors."

Interest. Enthusiasm. They can win for you. Sure you

need a knock-'em-dead presentation, but the winning edge can often be how excited you are about getting the business, how eager you are to work with the prospect's people, how strongly and sincerely you project your feelings.

But don't try to fake it. Your interest and enthusiasm must be real.

RULE NO. 18

Exploit the Q&A period

Effective handling of the question-and-answer session will enable you to nail down your key points.

Upfront, clarify whether you want questions held until the end or raised during the presentation. I prefer deferring them until the end to avoid interrupting the flow of the presentation. You could use a statement like: "Due to the time limits you've given us, we would ask you to hold your questions until the end...then we'll spend as much time as you want answering those questions." Of course, if someone insists on asking a question despite your request, it must be answered courteously.

A silent, unresponsive Q&A period can be embarrassing and deadly. Avoid this trap, if it occurs, by taking the initiative, asking rhetorical questions to address suspected "hidden" concerns, then answering them yourself. Some examples:

- "A question we frequently get is…"
- "Prospects usually want to know more about our capabilities in…"
- "Would it be helpful to you to learn more about how we would respond to…?"
- Or even "Bill, I'm sure we haven't answered all your concerns. What's on your mind?"

When questions come, answer them briefly and to the point, then reinforce a key point or customer benefit that derives from your response. Beyond that, observe how skilled politicians answer the initial question, then quickly move on to answer the question they wish had been asked.

Before responding, think quickly about the concern behind the query. Someone who asks about personnel turnover deserves more than a numerical answer; they may be skeptical about the stability of the firm or the continuity of personnel to be assigned to their account. Meet the real issue head-on.

Always test with each questioner whether you have answered the question to his/her satisfaction. If you don't know the answer, don't wing it. Reply that you will provide the information within 24 (or 48) hours — then be sure that you do.

The Q&A session should be like the final movement of a symphony summarizing all the main themes of your presentation in dramatic, convincing, upbeat fashion.

RULE NO. 19

Follow up religiously

The presentation may be over, but your campaign is still underway.

Immediately write a "Thank you" letter to everyone who listened to your presentation. My style was to have it on their desks the next morning.

Make the letter brief. Reinforce the key points of your presentation. Restate your interest and enthusiasm. Ask for the order. Express your sincere conviction that a positive decision in your favor will ensure their future progress and success.

Another effective technique is to provide additional information to an individual who asked a question — "Having thought about your question further I would like to amplify my answer." Then send copies to the other participants.

From experience we learned that periodic follow-up phone calls were perceived as evidence of genuine interest, not unwanted pestering. Make your calls brief, friendly, confident. If your calls are refused, there's always e-mail or creative mailings.

Rule No. 20

Celebrate your victory

Once you've received the happy news that you've won, take the first step toward the next successful presentation.

Celebrate your victory with your entire staff to create an aura of invincibility and build the belief that you're on a roll. Winning is contagious and can be a powerful catalyst for your next effort.

Make your celebration a big deal. Thank your colleagues who contributed to the win. Share the credit and the ownership. Announce (with obvious satisfaction) the rivals you beat. Position the win as the next critical advance in your relentless upward trajectory. Let your positive spirit infect your team.

Our approach was to stage a well-planned, spontaneous event (there's nothing more effective). As a total surprise, I rang a large ship's bell summoning everyone to the lobby to kick off the celebration, announced the win, thanked those responsible, named those to work on the business, under-scored its impact on our progress — all to great cheers and applause. Then we shared a glass of champagne together and toasted ourselves.

Everyone learns of the win at the same time. Everyone shares in the excitement. Esprit de corps gets a big lift. It's compensation for everyone's hard work — and it's a great team-building activity.

How to improve your odds

Building your approach and your presentation utilizing the preceding rules equips you with a strong game plan that will win most competitions.

*Yet there is a simple, little known but highly effective technique that will almost always outclass your rivals. This high-percentage strategy places critical emphasis on the work you do with your prospect **prior** to the actual presentation, so that the presentation itself becomes a fait accompli.*

Read on for the secret of this strategy.

A high-percentage game plan

There is a more effective presentation strategy than the dramatic "dog-and-pony show" or the well-staged "beauty contest."

It is simply to *sell your proposal before you make the presentation*. In this way the presentation itself is not a surprise or new information, but simply an affirmation of what the participants have already ratified.

The strategy depends on definitive fact-finding with *everyone* who will be on your selection committee. Here's what you need to learn:

- What are their goals and objectives — what do they want to achieve?

- What do they see as the opportunities and the obstacles?

- What kind of help do they want — what capabilities, what relationship, what responsibilities?

- What will be the decision criteria? (Get them to rank and weight these criteria). If criteria are not forthcoming, be ready to offer suggestions.

- What concerns do they have about a service firm or your proposal?

Armed with this on-the-ground intelligence, you can develop a precise, targeted presentation that punches home how you would help them succeed. But don't stop there.

Bounce your ideas off of a "friend within the walls" who can provide reactions and feedback. This is actually a dry run for your presentation. It can be invaluable in avoiding any landmines or booby traps that you may have innocently included. Or if you have not been able to talk to the president, you can get input to conform your presentation to his preferences.

It is a high-percentage approach since you go into the presentation with the confidence that you know what they want and with their vote almost in your pocket. Call it jury tampering — but in this case it's legal and effective.

How to ensure a winning edge

This Guide would not be complete without addressing four pragmatic areas that can deepen your knowledge base and sharpen your performance skills:

- *A concise summary that you should commit to memory.*
- *A valuable check list to help you hone your presentation*
- *Sixteen common mistakes to avoid*
- *Some final thoughts to round out your thinking about presentations*

Memorize this page

Here's a summary of a presentation strategy that will convince prospects that your proposal is the single best choice for them.

The core thought is to approach the final presentation as if you already had the account. Thus, you focus on *their* problems, your understanding of *their* problems, and your solutions to *their* problems. Instead of focusing on "why we're so great" you concentrate on "what we would do to help you succeed." This leverages the reality that they are far more interested in what you say about *them* than in what you say about *you* and *your* organization.

Fundamental to all this is the prospect perspective:

- Selecting a new professional service firm or launching a new initiative is an infrequent, unfamiliar task and hence a difficult decision.

- Prospects find it hard to translate *intangible* services into *tangible* benefits.

- They want the presentation to deal with *their* problems, *their* situation, and proposed solutions for *them*.

- They will often overemphasize the problem area they had with their previous service firm or program.

Preparing for this type presentation involves getting on the same wave length as the prospect by:

- Obtaining prospect input through their briefings, fact-finding, needs-analysis sessions with them, and digging into files and research reports they make available.

- Conducting field surveys or primary research to assess prospect vs. competition, preferences, obstacles.

- Doing a sweep of secondary data on the prospect, its situation and related factors via the Internet, media editors, industry experts.

- Working hard to develop personal rapport and avoiding know-it-all arrogance.

Armed with this information, you then structure a differentiated presentation to:

- Project your superior understanding of their situation and their goals.

- Explain how your research quantifies the options, relative difficulty, budget needs, and timeframe for reaching their goals.

- Delineate the problems, opportunities, and obstacles.

- Describe your recommended strategies and solutions that will result in success.

- Emphasize that start-up with them will be quick and easy, you're already ramped up on their situation, and ready to go to work.

The idea is simple, the preparation extensive, and the outcome will cause you to celebrate.

Checklist to enhance your presentation success

1. *Quietly pre-sell your **internal** audience*

   With an audience inside your organization, the presentation should almost be a formality. Prior to this event, you should have quietly talked to every participant individually, broached your ideas, asked for their input, listened to their objections, modified your proposition to get their buy-in, and thanked them for their support. (This tactic is expanded in A high-percentage game plan, page XX).

   Never go into a presentation cold. Go in knowing exactly what the outcome will be.

2. *Find the "hot button" for your **external** audience*

   You'll improve your chances for success if you pinpoint the key characteristic the prospect is seeking. Sure, they want quality, price and service, but what else? Specific experience, industry contacts, access to your top guys, big idea creativity, better teamwork, international resources, or what?

   Find out the basis for dissatisfaction with the previous outfit. Ask "dumb" questions. Look for a "friend within the walls" and debrief him. Check with third party vendors, referral network or the grapevine. Probe the prospect "What do I have to do to get your business?" Do some research.

   The "hot button" can be your key to victory.

3. *In meetings prior to the presentation, let the prospect "own the agenda."*

In meetings prior to the presentation, never launch immediately into your hard sell routine. Defer your agenda and let the prospect call the shots.

Make it clear that it is **their time** that is valuable and that they own the agenda. Suggest some options, be highly responsive and let them determine how to ensure effective use of their time.

Typically, the prospect will move directly to the issues that most concern them. Which is just what you want.

4. *Sell an intangible service by making it "tangible"*

Services are by definition intangible — one can't see, feel, taste, touch or often even hear them. They are usually customized to each client, produced on the spot, and delivered personally. Help the prospect appreciate your capabilities by making them as tangible as possible.

Our approach was to assume we already had the account and provide an extensive simulation of our workstyle during the presentation — presenting research, formulating strategies, showing creative ideas — all by the proposed account team. At the end we could say: "If you want to know what it's like to work with us, you've just had that experience with the actual team that will handle your business."

Finding ways to make your services tangible may require time and imagination. But it will pay off.

5. *Frame the decision process for the prospect*

   Counsel your prospect that their objective is not just to pick "a good firm." There are many good firms available to them in the marketplace. Their true objective is to select the firm with the best match between prospect **needs** and firm **capabilities**. Then demonstrate that you provide the best match, the best strategic fit with them.

6. *Use the presentation process to enhance the future relationship*

   The new business or client development process establishes the tone for the subsequent client-firm relationship. Therefore, it should be approached on a **peer-to-peer** basis characterized by confidence, openness, respect, good humor and sincere interest in the prospect individuals and the personal dimensions of their lives.

   If the prospect suggests or hints that they expect your subservience, bid them goodbye.

7. *Avoid future traps — never overpromise*

   Be realistic. Do not overpromise on what you can do for the prospect or what results you can reasonably deliver. It lays the groundwork for an early client loss.

   A familiar trap is to have your super-star people do a great dog-and-pony presentation, then assign down-the-line staffers to handle the account. When the client realizes he must deal with mere mortals, dissatisfaction arises shortly.

8. *Be a fanatic on prompt follow-up*

    After each meeting with the prospect, a personal let-
    ter should be sent immediately to each participant
    conveying your appreciation for his/her time and
    interest. Any unresolved issues or questions raised
    by the prospect should be answered within 48 hours
    or sooner.

    No meeting with a prospect should be permitted to
    terminate without obtaining agreement on the time
    and place of the next meeting. This displays your
    interest and keeps the interaction alive.

9. *Proactively provide a list of referral sources*

    Most prospects will want to check reference sources.
    Grab the initiative here by encouraging them to
    contact any of your clients or referral sources. Then
    proactively furnish them with a list including phone
    numbers of client individuals and references.

    They'll be reassured by your confidence and grati-
    fied by your anticipation of this request.

10. *Never be negative*

    Do not, under any circumstances, denigrate any
    competitor or say anything negative about any rival.

    Others may engage in mudslinging. Don't stoop to
    that tactic which is usually ineffective and displays
    some undesirable aspects about you. If a prospect
    bases the decision on negative information, it's
    probably someone you would not want as a client.

The winning approach: stand tall and accentuate the positive aspects and benefits of your firm.

11. *Be a winner*

The head of our Pittsburgh affiliate office coined some marvelous wisdom in his pungent statement: "No matter how much you want to win, never smell of desperation."

Think about it. People like to associate with winners. They like to work with successful individuals. And "being a winner" is often the deciding criterion in a close competition.

The lesson: Look like a winner. Dress like a winner. Act like a winner. Don't sweat!

12. *Never give up*

If you're not the winner, accept it graciously. But don't give up.

To make it a learning experience, ask for candid feedback on your presentation: What could you have done better? Where did you fall short? What did they like?

Maintain contact. Continue to display your interest aggressively. Track the work of your rival. Keep after them. After all you've made a sizable investment in this opportunity and it could pay off down the road.

Many new relationships falter quickly. New opportunities with this prospect may arise. A key player may move to another organization and give you a shot at their account.

Lots of things can change. In all these cases, you want to be waiting in the wings as an interested, legitimate contender.

Never let failure dent your confidence or diminish your optimistic outlook. Keep up the good fight.

The No-Nos

Avoid these common mistakes if you want to end up a winner.

1. **Don't** start talking as you make your way to your speaking position. Reach your position first, take a moment to get settled, scan your audience, then kick off your presentation.

2. **Don't** memorize your presentation word for word. It will come off as canned and stale. If you've done your homework, you know your material. Keep it fresh, change your pace to suit their reactions, let the words flow naturally.

3. **Don't** polish your presentation to the point that it becomes slick and superficial. Instead of giving a speech, have a conversation with your audience.

4. **Don't** focus exclusively on the big boss. Everyone has an ego, wants to feel important, and deserves some of your attention.

5. **Don't** insult anyone by mispronouncing his/her name. Find out ahead of time whether Mr. Smythe wants it to rhyme with "white" or "with."

6. **Don't** fall into the trap of using inane, juvenile cliches such as "you know what I mean?" or "do you get my point?"

7. **Don't** talk down to your audience. They may not be as smart as you are, but who wants to work with a know-it-all.

8. **Don't** betray your nervousness with distracting actions — fussing with your glasses, jiggling coins in your pocket, buttoning and unbuttoning your coat, clearing your throat repeatedly, picking lint off your sleeve, rocking back and forth, etc.

9. **Don't** apologize for any aspect of your presentation, your concepts, your organization, your track record. If you aren't ready to give it your best shot, stay home.

10. **Don't** assume *anything*! If you don't know for sure, find out or skip the subject. Bluffing is OK in poker, but not here.

11. **Don't** neglect to make sure that *everyone* can hear you and see your visuals.

12. **Don't** use "uh" and "um" to fill the empty space while you're thinking about your next point. Train yourself to keep quiet as you pause, or use some meaningful connective words like "where I want to go next is ____" or "that leads me to another benefit we offer."

13. **Don't** *ever* discuss politics or religion. These are no-win areas.

14. **Don't** forget to ask for the order. It displays your keen interest and requires a response.

15. **Don't** refer to "*if* we get your account" — always state it as "*when* we get your account." Then proclaim all the good things that will happen.

16. **Don't** forget to thank your audience for the opportunity, for their time and attention, and for their good questions.

Some Final Thoughts

A winning presentation is truly a high art form. It requires professional skills in speaking and acting, a keen sensitivity to your audience, a competitive product/service and great material.

A winning presentation is highly rewarding to you, your team and your organization. It justifies the time, money and resource investment you have made. It enhances morale. It sustains the upward momentum of the firm.

A winning presentation is a reality test which proves that you're good enough to prevail over your rivals.

A winning presentation recognizes that money only comes from outside your firm…and then provides the mechanism to go get that money.

A winning presentation gives you power, the power that derives from being able to attract and control "assets" for your firm.

A winning presentation produces an exhilarating high as you bask in the glow of victory.

A winning presentation deserves to be shared with your family whom you deserted during the preparation period. After winning, I always took the family out for an appreciation dinner which helped integrate family and work life.

A winning presentation means that you express your

deep appreciation to your new client, then promptly get to work to deliver on your promises.

A winning presentation is truly the lifeblood of an organization so let that transfusion add vitality, strength and optimism for the future.

Things to think about and do:

_____

_____

_____

_____

_____

_____

_____

_____

_____

_____

Things to think about and do:

_____

_____

_____

_____

_____

_____

_____

_____

_____

_____

_____

Things to think about and do:

Things to think about and do:

_____

_____

_____

_____

_____

_____

_____

_____

_____

_____

_____

Ordering Additional Copies

To order additional copies of this book please call

(800) 932-5420

or visit

www.greenleafbookgroup.com